The Hardest Day

Britain's Last Stand in the Second World War

Contents

INTRODUCTION – PRELUDE TO A BATTLE 1

CHAPTER 1: KENLEY & BIGGIN HILL 11

CHAPTER 2: STUKAS ARRIVE FOR LUNCH 22

CHAPTER 3: HORNCHURCH & NORTH WEALD......................................30

CHAPTER 4: THE MEDIA REACTION..37

CHAPTER 5: THE IMPORTANCE OF RADAR 45

CHAPTER 6: BRITISH & FOREIGN PILOTS, WOMEN ON THE GROUND..55

CONCLUSION – THE TIDE TURNS 65

BIBLIOGRAPHY..73

Introduction – Prelude to a Battle

After Hitler's ascension to power in 1933, Europe became increasingly alarmed as Germany shook off the shackles of the Treaty of Versailles, turned more militaristic, and set about conquering its neighbours. After the 1939 invasion of Poland, Britain and France declared war on Germany in the hopes of stopping Hitler's expansion across the continent. Yet when Hitler invaded France, his troops quickly bypassed their defences and they pushed French and British troops all the way back to Dunkirk and off the European mainland. Now, a German invasion of Britain was looming on the horizon.

Against this backdrop, Winston Churchill coined the term *Battle of Britain* in a speech delivered over the radio. Chomping on a cigar, and with an inability to pronounce his 's' sounds, his words fell on diffident ears, with one diarist even damning it as a really 'poor effort'. But Churchill, who was prone to bombast, painted a prophetic picture, one of free peoples being subsumed into a Nazi-inspired Dark Age. To keep the marauding forces of evil at bay, the English would have to defend their island tooth-and-nail and invoke the help of the United States. This was not empty rhetoric for Churchill – in a private dinner with his family, he instructed that each one had to kill one invading German, even if they had to use a simple kitchen knife to do it.

For a modern audience, one fully aware of Hitler's evil, Churchill's speech strikes the right tone. It is a dramatic call to arms just before a moment of historical reckoning. But before the sound of German planes roared over British cities, Churchill's resolve and moral certainty was out of chime with the popular mood. Not everyone wanted a war with Germany, and there is no evidence to suggest that the British public would not have followed another Prime Minister down the path of peace. And not only did Churchill the orator give a name to the Battle of Britain, he made it inevitable simply because he was determined to take the fight to an evil menace. But he had to win over the doubting masses. There were communists who felt a war would be a capitalist power struggle, the right-wing cabal who supported Hitler, and the pragmatists who, not unreasonably, felt Britain had no chance of beating the German war machine. Outside England, a few observers felt the same, notably the Americans, who Churchill wanted to woo, and Mahatma Gandhi, whose experience of British oppression pushed him to root for the Nazis. Churchill also had to navigate the divided political system that had placed him into the power at the expense of Neville Chamberlain, whose career had been ended by the promise of 'peace in our time'.

To win support, he used the only tool available to him – his voice. The power of his bombast was utilized to keep his plan to take on Hitler in motion. He was driven by an acute perception that Nazism was an evil force that he was duty bound to meet in battle, but he mixed this high-mindedness with facts. And to convince his people that England could repel a German invasion, he pointed to the RAF. He knew that the battle to save his homeland would be in the skies. He gave many a breathless speech about British planes hunting down the enemy, but his thoughts are best represented by this utterance:

When we consider how much greater would be our advantage in defending the air above this island against an overseas attack, I must say that I find in these facts a sure basis upon which practical and reassuring thoughts may rest.

But it was not only the British who were unsure of starting a war. The Germans, too, had their own reservations. Writing in *Mein Kampf*, Hitler praised the English for their history and their empire. The Austrian also acknowledged that Britain, historically, only wanted to maintain the balance of power in Europe, unlike the French, who Hitler saw as warmongering. He remained suspicious of Britain's willingness to enter battle for an abstract concept, as they had done in the First World War, when they declared war on behalf of the rights of small nations. Though, it must be said, the British empire was never a great defender of democracy. In practical terms, the Nazis wanted to cooperate with the English or neutralize their threat if an understanding could not be reached. If Europe could be secured, Hitler could then focus on the real prize – Russia. The Dictator wanted to conquer Russian lands for living space, but he also wanted to destroy communism and Judaism, which he felt were inextricably linked.

The German public, giddy on their army's uninterrupted success thus far, were impatient for British capitulation, and Hitler did not want to delay his invasion of Russia. From this cocktail of uncertainty and lack of conviction, it was decided that the Luftwaffe was the best way of pummelling the British. As outlined in Stephen Bungay's *The Most Dangerous Enemy: A History of the Battle of Britain*, this policy had three motivations: to make the threat of further invasion seem real; to weaken the RAF and heighten Britain's sense of vulnerability; and, lay the groundwork for a future siege. The Luftwaffe, like the German people, felt confident of victory.

The stage was being set for a confrontation between the RAF and the Luftwaffe, and many felt that the British were the underdogs. While German planes were truly devastating in their power, Nazi propaganda pushed the idea of an elite air force at every opportunity. Before the outbreak of the Second World War, the Germans even flew their limited fleet of planes to different airports around Germany, where they painted them different colours at each stop, took photographs with different pilots, some of whom were actually mechanics, to give the impression that the fleet was bigger than it actually was. In reality, in 1940, plane production in the UK was larger and more efficient than in Germany, principally because Hitler refused to use switch to a wartime economy until 1944.

Ironically, this propaganda had two negative consequences for the Nazis. Firstly, it made even Hitler overestimate the strength of his Luftwaffe, and it scared the British into taking the air defences seriously.

Staggeringly, even Hermann Goering did not have an idea of how many planes he had at his disposal. He was shocked when he learned of the true number before Operation Sealion was launched. He was also slow to realise that the planes that had been lost in other campaigns had not been replaced. To make matters worse, the Luftwaffe were expected to shoot down 100 British planes a week, which was optimistic, to say the least. Weather could curtail raids; German pilots would have to be consistently accurate to a high degree, which was not guaranteed; and British planes would have to obligingly present themselves as targets, which was not going to happen. In addition, the limited range of the German planes meant only the south coast of England could be attacked, which meant that RAF planes could recuperate out of the firing line, in England's northern part.

On the other hand, despite Britain's fear of the Luftwaffe, their plan to counteract it was uneven, which potentially gave an advantage to the Germans.

According to Michael Korda's analysis in *With Wings like Eagles: The untold story of the Battle of Britain,* the system for training pilots, especially as the Battle of Britain progressed, was deeply flawed, out of date and resistant to change. Many of the new recruits were barely 17 and were given their planes after only a few hours of training. The pilot course had been shortened to meet the demand of training all the new pilots. To compound this situation, they were not trained in deflection shooting – meaning, anticipating the trajectory of an enemy plane and shooting the bullets so the targeted plane flew into the bullets – or other techniques that might make their jobs easier and safer. They were given words of advice, such as never fly straight and level for more than 20 seconds, but the chaos of battle came as a shock to the young men, whose new airborne lives were measured in minutes. Such was the inexperience of some of the youngsters, some veteran pilots were as scared of their own wingmen as they were of the Luftwaffe. It was a fear shared by experienced German pilots when they had to fly with their own raw recruits.

In one alarming situation on The Hardest Day, a new pilot and his team in the 501 Squadron were suddenly surrounded by a group of Messerschmitts. The experienced pilots broke right in evasive maneuvres, but the new pilot, who was checking to see if his gun was on, missed it and was left stranded. Somehow, he survived.

These British pilots would be tested to limit by the constant waiting and frenetic dogfights. Many were caught up in events bigger than themselves and focused on simply doing their job. For the Luftwaffe, Scott Isle's in-depth study, *More than 'an enemy's name, rank and number': Information gained from Luftwaffe prisoners of war and its use for British intelligence during the Battle of Britain, July – October 1940*, reveals how German bomber and fighter pilots were sometimes at odds with one another, and how morale could be affected by poor leadership and political interference from the Nazi Party.

The Heinkel He 111 was the main plane used by the Luftwaffe. It had a bomb load up to 1,500 kg and had a 4-5-man team. It had a streamlined design, but the pilot had poorer visibility. The Dornier D17 was a light bomber designed to outrun chasing fighter planes. It manoeuvred easily at low altitudes, allowing the plane to be highly effective when it came to surprise bombing attacks. Its crew of four was protected by the smaller frame of the plane, which made it harder to hit. This plane also had a unique cooling system, which made it less vulnerable to enemy fire. Finally, the Stukas had a two-man crew and three bombs, a 250 kg one under the fuselage, and a 50 kg bomb under each wing. The

Stuka was practically invulnerable to attack while it was diving – it simply moved too fast. Yet after the bomber inevitably pulled up out of its dive, it became easier to hit.

The British Spitfire was a fast machine powered by a Merlin engine, and it was designed so it could climb quickly and intercept enemy bombers. Owing to the peculiar design of its wing, which was elliptical, it performed well even at high altitudes. The Hurricane fighter was more widely used than the Spitfire during the Battle of Britain, and it registered more kills. Despite its more conventional design and relative lack of pace, its series of guns were devastating when turned against German bombers. In addition, it was easily fixed after battle so it could be quickly put back up into the sky.

All the while, normal life was being interrupted by the creeping signs of approaching battle. It was a time when even the railings outside homes were melted down, to be used, in the words of a 15-year-old Londoner, to make 'battleships or something'. Tim Clayton and Phil Craig's *Finest Hour* also details how, with German aggression against Britain imminent, children were being sent to Canada; some were thrilled because they conflated Canada with the United States of America, and that meant cowboys, Indians, and movie stars.

With all these factors in the balance, the Battle of Britain eventually started on July 10, and it had four distinct phases. The first phase lasted until August 12th, and it saw German bombs falling on Channel shipping and numerous night raids; the second phase was an intense 5-day-period, which lasted until the 18th, and was marked by Luftwaffe attacks on airfields and radar stations; the third phase saw heavy bombing of British cities and airfields, between August 19th and September 6th; finally, mass bombing raids were launched against London and other major cities, which lasted until the end of October. This final part of the campaign was an act of desperation prompted by the Luftwaffe's inability to knock the RAF's radar stations and airfields out of action. Ultimately, the Nazi bid to break the spirit of the English by bombing urban centres also ended in failure.

Throughout these 4 phases, there were a number of significant dates. August 13th was Eagle Day, the first day of Operation Eagle Attack. The entire operation was a significant juncture in the air war. Had the RAF fallen to the Luftwaffe attacks, a land invasion would have been the next step. Confusion, however, reigned from the start, and confirmation for the operation was only given after the first bombers had taken off. In fact, it had been originally called off because of bad weather, but this information had not been given to the German pilots. Many of these bombers were successfully intercepted because the British were using a sophisticated radar system, and very few targets were destroyed.

West Malling, an airfield, was hit on the 16th. A raid on Hornchurch was foiled by bad weather and the RAF's 54 Squadron. Elsewhere, bombs were dropped on Surrey and Wimbledon, while 266 Squadron engaged the enemy, but it was a disaster because they lost 4 Spitfires. Two squadron leaders were killed. Heny La Fone Greenshields was with them, and pursued the Germans to Calais, where he was shot down over a sandbank. They found a letter in his pocket that spoke of how he had been bombed at Eastchurch, which fuelled the Nazi's false belief that this Coastal Command Base was important.

The most important attack of the day was a lunchtime raid by Stukas at Tangmere. It was intercepted by 8 British squadrons, but buildings were still hit, and water and power supplies were cut. 14 planes undergoing repair on the ground had to be written off. 8 Stukas also hit Ventnor radar station. Goering did not think it was not that important but allowed the raid anyway. Two planes feigned that they were going to land, hoping to fool the people at the base. It worked, and they managed to destroy a few grounded training planes.

General Hastings Ismay, a close aide to Winston Churchill, described being 'sick with fear' after seeing all the squadrons engaged during those afternoon attacks, and wave after wave of German planes. After visiting the Uxbridge Operations Room with Churchill, the Prime Minister was in a daze and in no mood to talk to Ismay. Finally, he turned to the General and uttered the historic words he would later repeat in the House of Commons: 'Never in the field of human combat of has so much been owed by so many to so few'. But the raids continued on the 17th, and bombs fell on Wimbledon, with only the tennis courts suffering damage. Pilot Officer W. M. L. 'Billy' Fiske becomes the first American killed in the Battle of Britain; he was twice the captain of the US bobsled team at the Olympics and he was well-liked by his colleagues.

Even though the Battle of Britain would rumble on until October 31st, the intensity of Luftwaffe attacks on strategic targets culminated on August 18th, The Hardest Day. The RAF faced three bombing raids in the late morning, lunchtime, and evening. It was Hermann Goering's bold roll of the dice, an intense gambit to bend the Battle of Britain to his will. It failed. In one of his most famous speeches, Churchill promised to defend England in the streets and on the beaches, but he never had to make good on his promise. The bravery of RAF pilots and the Women's Auxiliary Airforce (WAAF) plotters, the use of radar, German failures and large dollops of luck elided into a qualified victory for the British on The Hardest Day. The German invaders were pushed back, which offered a hopeful sign that the Nazis, and all the repugnant things they stood for, could be overcome.

CHAPTER 1:
Kenley & Biggin Hill

August 18th began with little cloud cover, with plays opening in theatres, advertisements for winter clothes in newspapers, and Adolf Hitler planning to spend a quite Sunday in the Alps. It was also a day of three Luftwaffe attacks on England. By the nightfall, both sides would suffer their heaviest day of lost or destroyed planes. No other day in the Battle of Britain, before or after the 18th, surpassed the damage incurred on what is justifiably known as The Hardest Day.

Early morning saw reconnaissance missions, which went largely undetected until 11 AM when one lone reconnaissance plane was tracked and intercepted by the RAF. The German plane thought that it was too high to be attacked, but it was chased across the Channel until it was forced to crash into the sea. The intelligence gathered by these planes was patchy, and German fighters and bombers headed for England expecting little resistance. They seriously underestimated how many planes the RAF had, believing that the RAF only had 300 serviceable planes, and they did not even have a good idea of which airfields housed which type of plane. This was a fatal oversight. In reality, 800 planes and 280 reserve pilots were waiting for them. The German's could not know either that Churchill had prioritized the development of UPs (unrotated projectiles) – these were like smaller, sneakier versions of a barrage balloon, and they worked by hitting into an enemy plane and forcing it to crash.

But these were not the only dangers. The German plan for the whole day was inherently risky. The Luftwaffe had never before sent so many bombers so deep into English territory, and its afternoon raids would see more Stukas committed than ever before. Yet German morale was high, and several authors point to a letter written by the pilot Hans-Otto Lessing to his parents on the day before the grand assault. He claimed the 'British are getting weaker' and he was sure of victory. Lessing's subsequent death on the 18th was a tragic symbol of the misplaced confidence which undermined every facet of the German plan.

The first attacks were planned for late morning on the airbases of Kenley and Biggin Hill. Kenley was home to 64 Squadron with Spitfires and 615 Squadron with Hurricanes. It had a staff of 30 officers, 600 airmen, and 100 airwomen. To protect the base, there was a complement of infantry men, anti-aircraft gunners, whose job was exceedingly difficult, and an assortment of anti-aircraft guns. Planes were not typically stored in the hangars, as they were an obvious target, and the sick bay intentionally did not have a red emblazoned on the roof. The planes were dispersed around a concrete perimeter with intermittent blast walls, designed for added protection. These had only been added in the early part of 1940.

Biggin Hill was 16 minutes flying time for the Germans – the worry was that the Nazis would fly in low, avoiding radar until they were quite close to their target, catching the British pilots stationed there unawares.

Kenley airbase was to be attacked in three phases, with each one separated by just a few minutes respite. First, its hangars would be taken out by high-flying bombers. In the second wave, other bombers were expected to carpet bomb the runways. Finally, low-flying planes coming in from the south-west were expected to precision bomb anything that was left standing.

This was a new tactic, one designed to force British planes into open combat. Early in the Battle of Britain, German fighters had successfully provoked the RAF into fighting by sending 'free hunting' patrols. The British initially took the bait, but after suffering heavy losses, they became more reluctant to engage these patrols. The Nazis believed that bombing specific targets would inveigle the RAF into a dogfight. This was not a fool-proof strategy. In these bombing raids, German bombers had to be closely escorted by Messerschmitt fighters, a situation hated by all fighter as it limited their ability to fight on the front foot. In addition, the Messerschmitt had quite a limited range, meaning it could only engage in battle over a short period of time. For pilots heading from Cherbourg, as was the case for the later lunchtime attacks, they were exposed to biting cold, which was a serious problem, and the twin, mortal terror of the water and Spitfire. Collectively, this was known as 'Channel Fear'. Thus, the plan had technical pitfalls and it relied on the men holding their nerve.

German pilots were working off detailed photos, specific targets and assigned approaches. Yet nobody in German intelligence spotted the Operations room in Kenley or Biggin Hill on these maps, a detail which shows that reconnaissance photos, which were taken from a great height, lacked resolution. They were wooden structures and hard to spot, while the Germans also could not notice that they were connected to other Operation rooms by underground cables. In general, the Nazis underestimated their importance; while destroying runways and planes disrupted the RAF, the Operations room was part of a sophisticated network which coordinated the response of the RAF on a sector-by-sector basis, which meant that different bases had the freedom to organize their own response to incoming Nazi aircraft. And the British were well prepared. If Kenley's nerve centre had been hit, coordinating British planes in that sector would have been moved to a butcher shop a mile away.

Michael Korda, in *With Wings Like Eagles: The Untold Story of the Battle of Britain*, gives a great insight into what life was like in these bases. Pilots could wait by their planes sunbathing or playing cards, waiting for a phone call to come through and the shouted command: 'scramble!'. The ringing of the phone was enough to make some of the men vomit, and the ominous sound of a phone call stayed with them for years. The dispersal hut saw the upper classes mixing freely with officers who had flown many times; the atmosphere was that of a locker room, where the boys also passed the time by reading risqué thrillers or looking at the travails of a blonde bombshell in a newspaper comic strip. Despite her best efforts, her clothes kept coming off, and Churchill considered her scantily clad physique as a great morale booster for the pilots and the nation.

Edith Heap was about to clock off in the Debden Operations Room when she heard her headphones crackle with the sound of a human voice. A 'hostile' had been spotted, and soon that solitary enemy became an estimated 350 enemies spread across half-a-dozen different raids. In normal circumstances, it could be difficult to determine if an imminent raid was real or just a feint; getting it wrong could be a waste of petrol and could see the planes on the ground when the real attack came. But on August 18th, the magnitude of the German attack was understood almost immediately.

While the high-altitude attackers were following the Folkestone-Reigate railway, which almost went as far as Kenley, low-flying Dornier bombers were coming in over the south coast of England. As they flew, they were fired upon by Royal Navy patrol boats. The British sailors were probably close enough to see the pilots wearing specially designed steel helmets, which was worn by any pilot flying at a low altitude because they were more vulnerable to ground fire. The German bombers replied to the bullets of the Royal Navy with a burst of ineffectual machine gun fire. They had also been spotted by the Observer Corps, so Kenley had advance warning of their approach. Plotters donned their helmets and anti-aircraft guns faced the skies expectedly, though some of Kenley's staff took little heed of the warning as they ate lunch on the grass or ambled in the sun.

Onlookers on the ground in different parts of England saw how easily German bombers evaded anti-aircraft fire and then they heard those bombers drop their load further inland. For people who had not seen or heard the Germans, the fact that the BBC had stopped broadcasting would have aroused their suspicions. In fact, Hatfield transmitter had been turned off so that the Germans could not use it as a beacon. As the German bombers flew low over British town and villages, people looking up from the sky did not immediately register that the planes were German. After a few moments, the distinctive crosses on the wings pushed the people below into recognition of the enemy and to find cover. Those planes flying low over England's south coast had also been spotted by civilians when they reached landfall, and one couple working in their garden noted the sinister air of these intruding machines. All in all, seeing these planes as they brushed tree-tops and cast shadows over town streets and country lanes inspired great fear in the people below. In one act of random violence, one German machine gun peppered a fires station, sending people scurrying for safety. There were no casualties.

As the raid over Kenley began, a pilot in one of the Dorniers was hit in the chest. In *The Most Dangerous Enemy*, Bungay explains how he slid forward and exclaimed, 'Get me home!'. His navigator had to take control of the plane, but the badly damaged aircraft crash landed near Biggin Hill. These precision bombers quickly realized that, instead of being the last to arrive, they were actually the first. Owing to the bad weather, which was getting worse as the day wore on, the cohesion and battle order was disrupted, with the attack running slightly behind schedule. The guns at Kenley were firing on the planes, and the Dorniers replied with canon and machine gun fire. The sky was ablaze with bullets and there was a noxious smell of phosphorous in the air.

The RAF scrambled almost 100 planes. The force was split between planes protecting the skies of Margate and Cantebury, and the planes directly defending Kenley and Biggin Hill. Despite being attacked by 111 squadron, the Dorniers dropped their bombs on Kenley; some of these bounced on the runways and caused significant damage to Kenley's installations. As the Dorniers flew off, soldiers on the ground fired parachute and cable launchers at them. This weapon was Winston Churchill's aforementioned pet project. At least one Dornier was pulled from the sky, killing all 5 men on board. For people on the ground, the sight of parachutes convinced them that German were invading with ground troops, proving that these devices had the capacity to surprise and terrify both friend and foe alike.

Squadron Leader Mike Crossley was leading 12 Hurricanes in 32 Squadron when he noticed the second wave of German attackers. He was heard to shout 'Tally-ho' in order to alert those down below that he was engaging the enemy. He and his men had long theorized that flying directly at the Germans was an effective tactic when it came to breaking up enemy formations, and now they had the perfect opportunity to put this theory into practice. One of his lieutenants was determined to take out the bombers because his pregnant wife was below, but the Hurricanes were forced to change tactics when they were suddenly flanked by the German escorts.

In Tim Clayton and Phil Craig's *Finest Hour*, we learn that 501 squadron were flying back to base on their day off when they heard the news of the attack. While still trying to absorb the breaking information, a German fighter pilot emerged from the sun, and in one effortless sweep, shot down four British planes. This German was flying with the rest of his squadron, but he told them to remain up in the clouds. A single aircraft could find a firing position without being detected but a larger force would have been spotted. More of the 502 Squadron could have been downed by the German, but debris from one of the British planes hit his plane, forcing a retreat.

This second wave, comprising of Hienkels, despite attention from Crossley's squadron, eventually arrived and dropped their bomb load as well. The resulting smoke made precision bombing the hangars impossible. When the planes responsible for this part of the raid arrived, which due to the disorder of the operation, was now the last part of the attack, they went instead to the secondary target of West Malling. 601 squadron were finding it hard to break through the bomber escorts at Kenley and the Hienkels and the bombers that bombed West Malling turned for home after dropping their loads, but the RAF planes patrolling Margate and Cantebury were lying in wait. After fanning out, they hit the retreating Germans hard over Kent and the English Channel. Rudolf Lamberty's Dornier was badly hit, and his left wing was on fire. Lamberty could feel the heat because it was so intense, and he was set upon by more than one British plane. The rest of the crew in the plane jumped out and injured themselves as they jumped from a low height, and the pilot was forced into crash landing after rifle fire from the Home Guard damaged it from below. Lamberty managed to escape from the burning wreck and surrender. He was treated well enough by the English civilians, even if one accidentally opened his parachute. He even surprised them by showing them his pack of English cigarettes.

In this phase of retreat and counterattack by the RAF, the battle was fierce for both sides. Once the British planes were forced to break off after firing on the Germans, the underside of the plane was exposed. In addition, one-by-one, the chasing Hurricanes ran out of ammunition and were forced to turn for home. The weather, which had done so much to hinder the German attacks, also inhibited the British response. In sunnier skies, more RAF planes could have been put into action against the withdrawing Luftwaffe, but the hazy weather resulted in less planes being used in the pursuit.

One British pilot was forced to eject from his plane and waited a full minute before releasing his parachute. He had heard the Germans had started shooting at parachuting pilots, and he was not going to take any chances. Unfortunately, he did not know how to free fall properly, and when he landed dizzily, an old man pulled a gun on him, convinced that he was a German. Passing soldiers rescued him from the confusion. When he was brought to a nearby golf course for a rest, the posh golfers ignored him and occasionally rebuked him because the sound of warring planes had ruined their game.

Alfred Price wrote *Battle of Britain: Summer of Reckoning*, and he describes how Sergeant Elizabeth Mortimer was working at Biggins when the alarm was sounded. In her own words, she was enjoying a cup of tea in the mess when the loudspeaker told them to take cover. They ran to the nearest shelter, but nothing happened, so they returned to their still warm tea. This pattern repeated a few more times. By the fourth alarm, they were fed up and moved slowly to safety. Once outside the mess, they saw German planes heading right for them, which was enough to quicken their sluggish pace toward the shelter.

Elaine Lewis was a plotter in the Biggins Hills Operations Room, and she 'felt a strange feeling' as the German planes came closer. Eventually, the sound of bombs in the distance grew louder until they were ordered to take cover under a big table. There was a loud smash; the glass where they plotted their squadrons was blown into pieces that flew all over the room, into hair and clothing.

The bombing here was more conventional, though, and many of the bombs fell far from their intended targets, over woods and fields, which startled some of the people who had run to the woods for cover. The German bombers were untroubled by flak from the ground as they made their approach, and many of the pilots pondered whether the British lacked the capacity to fight and continue the Battle of Britain. After the raid on Biggin, a WAAF member defused an unexploded German bomb and subsequently became the first woman in the Battle of Britain to be awarded the Military Medal for courage. This medal was commonly referred to as a 'man's medal'. In our enlightened times, women having such an active role in military life is not a remarkable detail, but the 1940s belonged to another world. There were serious reservations over how women would react to being bombed, and they were always expected to act according to strict gender codes. One WAAF recruit was reprimanded for swearing like a trooper, until her persistent potty mouth eventually made her superiors laugh. Once they showed their mettle in the heat of bombing raids, they won respect from the men and sexism became less of an issue as the Battle of Britain developed.

Both Kenley and Biggin Hill survived the rapid onslaught. Despite the heavy bombing, they were still operational, and Biggin Hill came out of it relatively unscathed, though with 2 dead and no airplanes damaged. Kenley, on the other hand, saw the sick bay and 3 hangars destroyed, with a few people dead. The burning hangars were hard to put out and there was the issue of the unexploded bombs; they were dropped from a low altitude and failed to explode. Nevertheless, within minutes of the attack, it was able to receive, repair and refuel planes and a reserve transmitter was put to work. The Germans were not finished, however, and a large group of Stuka bombers were preparing to cross the Channel. The RAF was going to be kept busy.

CHAPTER 2:
Stukas Arrive for Lunch

In the middle of the action over Kenley and Biggin Hill, a reconnaissance plane was feeding information to another bombing party, one which included Stukas. The group rendezvoused over Cherbourg, and this force of 109 dive bombers headed for England at around lunchtime. At the Isle of Wight, the Stukas headed east in order to precision bomb Gosport, Thornley Island, Ford, and radar station Poling.

Tim Clayton and Phil Craig's *Finest Hour* does a great job of explaining how reconnaissance photos of the different sites, as was the case with the Kenley and Biggin Hill raids, were taken from a great height because they were aggressively chased off by the RAF, which meant that even though the Germans knew these 4 places were active, they did not know the what type of planes were on the ground. Thus, the Germans mistakenly believed that the RAF was using the three airfields to scramble Hurricanes and Spitfires during the Battle of Britain. In actual fact, Gosport, which would be attacked by 22 Stukas. was home to a torpedo development unit, while Thornley Island

and Ford were both concerned with coastal and naval defence, and both of these sites were attacked by 28 Stukas. Poling was attacked with the biggest force, with 31 Stukas trying to take out its radar installations.

This large force of bombers would fly over the Channel as one giant mass, defended in the process by 157 Messerschmitt fighters. It was so big, it both shocked and awed people looking up from English towns and villages because the planes flew in disciplined formation, with only daylight between the wingtips of different planes. Poling detected the approaching formation and scrambled 68 fighters from 5 different airfields on the south coast, which gave the Germans a 4:1 advantage in terms of the numbers of planes in the sky. The plotters in this station knew a large force was arriving, but they greatly underestimated the actual size of this raid, but it is doubtful that more RAF planes would have been committed had the real number been known. The other airborne planes were coming back to base after defending Kenley and Biggin Hill, and they desperately needed rearming and refuelling.

Arthur Price's *The Hardest Day*, like in the preceding chapter, is full of engaging personal anecdotes for each phase of the attacks on August 18th. For the Stuka attacks, he tells the story of Flight Lieutenant Dunlop Arie, whose squadron was enjoying a well-earned break when they were called into action. Leaving his beer behind, Arie and his men ran back to base, but to the young man's horror, his Spitfire was not ready for action. Spotting a freshly delivered Spitfire, he jumped in that instead, even though the sights had not been harmonized with the guns. But now, 602 Squadron could fly and meet the aggressors.

The German bombers arrived at Ford, Gosport and Poling without meeting much RAF resistance. The skies over these stations, however, would be later filled with hundreds of planes, creating utter chaos.

At Poling, WAAF Corporal Joan Avis Hearn was working when the order to take cover came in, but she felt compelled to continue working because of the large group of enemy planes. Operators from other radar stations were trying to get in touch because they knew the Stukas were heading straight for Hearn's position. The lines went dead but she could hear the whistle of bombs and the sound of planes as they attacked. Nearby, a family heard the terrific din of Stuka engines and had nothing but the roof of their house and saucepans on their head to protect them; they could hear the sound of the exploding bombs at Poling, and the rat-a-tat of machine gun fire as the Stukas covered their rear.

At Ford, only 6 Lewis guns were on hand to defend the people and infrastructure. The all-clear had been given at this station, so the appearance of enemy bombers came as a great surprise. Bombs fell on the hangars, grounded planes and barrack huts, while a huge fire was started when Ford's fuel storage was hit. Heroically, one man on the ground was killed as he fired his revolver in desperation at the incoming planes. He was cut to pieces by the Germans, and his hand was later found, still holding the gun tightly.

Gosport saw the Spitfires of 234 Squadron quickly shoot down 3 Messerschmitts, one of which had been chased down to sea level, where it subsequently crashed into the water. For the bombers, however, they were relatively untroubled by British planes as they began their dives. In a flash, they dropped their load and rose back into the sky.

The bombers over Thornley Island were less fortunate, and they lost 6 planes in just 2 minutes. 43 and 601 Squadrons, a force made up of 18 Hurricanes, attacked the Stukas as they began preparing for their dives. One British pilot flew at 5 Stukas, firing at each one in turn. He saw the crew bale out of 2 of those planes. Bill Pond of 601 Squadron was chasing a Stuka, whose rear gun was scoring hits on his Hurricane. This resulted in his windscreen turning black with oil from his engine. Knowing that German escort fighters would enter the fray at any moment, he pulled out of the battle, which was a normal course of action because he was a sitting duck with such limited visibility.

Guenther Meyer-Bothling was flying one of the Stukas and he was hit in the head by a Hurricane bullet. Then he was hit in the thigh by another bullet. His radio operator was dead and he, like Pond, dived out of the melee. As he tended to his head wound, he tried and failed to jettison his bombload. On the defender's side, Frank Carey had also been hit in the leg. Feeling faint and dizzy, he decided to land rather than risk fainting mid-air. He chose an open field, but unbeknownst to him, hidden trenches had been dug in order to destroy any German plane that decided to land there. Carey learned first-hand that the tactic worked, and his Hurricane buckled and crashed once it made contact with ground. It was a rough landing for this 'Halton brat', who joined the RAF at 15-years-old and then fought with distinction through the entirety of World War II.

Near Thornley Park, housewife Amelia Sop was eating her lunch under the stairs in the midst of roaring engines and the fury of war. The sound of shouting lured her outside to her kitchen window, where she could see her next-door neighbour shouting at her little boy to get off the garden shed. He was cheering the British planes while the mother was trying to protect herself from bombs by covering her head with an apron. The absurdity made Amelia laugh hysterically.

All along the coast, bombers and dive bombers were attacking stations. 234 squadron defended the South Coast in planes with a striking insignia – a Spitfire emblazoned across a broken Swastika. Bob Doe was in one of these planes, and he hunted down two German Messerschmitt. In one, the canopy flew off and he could see the face of his blonde enemy. This face-to-face encounter spooked Doe, forcing him into not shooting more at the German. The Messerschmitt crashed into the sea, more than likely claiming the life of its pilot on the process.

As the Stukas headed for home, British Hurricane fighters followed them. The Stukas were famously slow and outgunned, which handed the RAF an advantage. Karl Henze's Stuka had been damaged and his Stuka lost even more speed – he was being overtaken by everybody, and with each passing second, he became an attractive target for any British plane. He was soon set upon by one, and he engaged in defensive maneuvres and flew low, trying to narrow the angle of his pursuer's shooting. Miraculously, he bounced off the top of the water and back into the air, with the British pilot nowhere to be seen. This was a double stroke of luck – normally, hitting the water like Henze did flips the plane, while the plane that had been chasing him probably ran out of ammunition. He survived, but the Stukas were not faring well. A radio operator in another Stuka could see smoking bombers all around him. Ultimately, 15 Stukas were shot down, with another 7 damaged beyond repair.

Julius Neumann's Stuka crashed pretty much intact, according to Price's book. On his descent, he wondered what his final message should be. Since he had no family, he considered shouting something for Hitler, but decided against it in case it sounded too forced or trite. Instead, he maintained radio silence and survived the impact into British soil. Emerging shaken but alive from his ordeal, he lit a cigarette and waited for someone to find him as he had nothing better to do.

But the Messerschmitt escorts were not giving up the fight, and they set about counter-attacking the Spitfires. 602 Squadron lost 4 planes in quick succession, with a Spitfire having to crash land in the cemetery of a local town. On his descent, he also crashed into some power lines and cut their electricity for a few hours. He was so angry when he emerged from his cockpit, the normally mild-mannered Scot was mistaken for being Polish as he left off a string of imaginative swear words.

It was not uncommon for an RAF pilot to shoot down the enemy and then discover he had a German on his tail, and in the middle of it all, British fighters tried to avoid colliding into one another and the dangers of friendly fire. There was danger on all sides, but eventually the fighting ceased, and calm was again, temporarily at least, restored.

Smoke from Ford could be seen for miles around, and to some onlookers, the huge ball of flame looked inextinguishable, while one solider in the Home Guard found the sight to be heart-breaking. Touring Ford after the raid was a grisly experience because there were dead bodies and burning buildings everywhere. In the showers, one naval youth had been killed by a falling bomb while he was taking a bath. He was found naked and almost cut in half. Ambulance crews and first-aid crews rushed to the scene, and Price details some remarkable moments of heroism. Wren Steward Nina Marsh tended to everyone else before looking after her own injuries, and this selflessness was repeated by others at Ford, with people more concerned about others than their own welfare.

The informative YouTube channel, The Operations Room, made a great video on the all parts of August 18th. Entitled *The Hardest Day, Battle of Britain – Time-lapse*, their conclusion for what happened at Ford is that the damage was significant, but not strategically important. There was significant loss of life because the Germans attacked with little warning, but they also they wrongly assumed that Ford was a command centre, so the wasted resources in trying to destroy it. A number of seaplanes were put out of action, but there were not any Spitfires or Hurricanes on the ground at Ford.

Poling's radar station was put out of action, but this was simply a minor inconvenience for the British. The low-level radar was still working, and they set up a temporary station to supplement the radar coverage, but there no real gaps in the network as there were a number of regional stations still scanning the skies for signs of enemy activity. Thornley Island lost a couple of hangars and planes, and Gosport lost some buildings, hangars and planes, but it suffered no loss of life.

Both of the airfields at Gosport and Thornley Island continued to operate, though with some limitations.

The weather had again worked in the RAF's favour, with the haze making it difficult for Messerschmitts to coordinate their defense of the Stuka bombers. But the British learned a chastening lesson of what happens when a site is bombed with little warning, as happened in the case of Ford. Overall, the Germans had little to show for their attacks on the 18th. There would be time for two more raids in the evening, 150 miles to the east.

CHAPTER 3:
Hornchurch & North Weald

The late afternoon they saw the third main attack of the day. 58 Dorniers and 53 Hienkels approached airfields at Hornchurch and North Weald, escorted by 150 Messerschmitts. Multiple squadrons of Spitfires and Hurricanes were scrambled to intercept. There were 47 Spitfires and 96 Hurricanes in the air to meet the enemy, meaning there were 3 British planes for every 5 German fighters and bombers. This time, the plotter's estimation of how many German aircraft were in English skies was pretty much accurate, but the defenders were still outnumbered. According to Price's other book, *Battle of Britain: A Summer of Reckoning*, Flying Officer Innes Westmacott gulped as he saw the size of the German raid. During the air battle, he later remembered that masses of German planes seemed to be after him. After failing to hide in a cloud, he launched into a ferocious dive, one which helped shrug off his German attackers.

32, 54, 56, and 501 Squadrons went toward to the Margate-Cantebury Line to engage the enemy first, while the rest of the units were instructed to climb to a high altitude and to see how the battle was playing out before intervening. 56 Squadron was split into 4 parts – 3 were charged with taking out the bombers, and 1 section was reserved for the escorts. The fighters escorting the bombers heading for North Weald were in a dangerous situation because they had to slow their speed and stick close to their bombers. This limitation is wonderfully illustrated by The Operations Room in their time lapse of The Hardest Day.

We learn in Clayton and Craig's *Finest Hour* that Edith Heap heard once more the sound of 'hostile' across the radio waves, and the operations headquarters was a confusing babble of orders, chat between the pilots and the fearful cries of the headquarters staff as they observed the battles from a distance. There was incredible commotion, but humorous stories still shine true. One family allegedly ran for the nearest hill rather than cover to see the dogfights, binoculars at hand, while an old man told an American journalist with a smile that the German bombs had missed the village pub.

Flight Lieutenant Edward Gracie led a section of planes toward the bombers, but he was kept at bay by the German escorts. This situation was repeated on the second attack, but proving that third time is a charm, the last sweep gave Gracie and his unit of Hurricanes the opportunity to fire at the bombers. While Gracie's men were keeping the escorts busy, other sections of 56 Squadron positioned themselves at the bomber's rear, which resulted in one Heinkel being shot down. They were soon joined by 54 Squadron, and the melee became even larger. Pilot Officer Colin Gray, a New Zealander, was with 54 Squadron, and he was able to fire at a few Messerschmitts before running out of ammunition. Another Pilot Officer in this squadron was 'John Willie' Hopkin, and he also scored a few hits.

Down below, at street level, in the civilian world, a wedding was taking place. The bride and groom were strolling outside, seeking to escape their respective families for a brief moment. When they spotted the bombers and fighters, they ran to the reception hall, where the ensuing sound of roaring engines and machine gun fire cowed the guests and made them seek comfort in each other's arms. The palpable fear was ramped up by the sound of the plane that crashed near the church. Colin Gray saw the explosion, and as Price tells us in *The Hardest Day*, the Kiwi knew that it was one Messerschmitt that would not make it back home. When he died in 1995, the obituary in the *Independent* hailed him as one of the best pilots in the entire Battle of Britain.

In a remarkable incident, a Heinkel was badly damaged and spiralled into a descent, desperately looking for a place to crash land. The rest of the crew were badly injured, so the pilot knew there was no chance to bail out. All the way down, a British fighter escorted it down without firing; it was an act of chivalry in the midst of a ferocious day of fighting. There are other examples on the 18th that speak of people's better nature, and more than one shot-down German had his wounds tended to by ordinary British people. This invariably came as a surprise to some of the downed German pilots, as they had heard rumours that British civilians went around beating them up. There are examples of this brutality happening, but it was not a widespread practice.

These Spitfires and Hurricanes were running out of ammunition, but by now it was clear that the German force was heading for North Weald. In response, 46, 85, 151, 257, and 310 Squadrons were ordered to intercept them. At the same time, another force was heading for Hornchurch, and 32 and 501 Squadrons tried to meet them, but they were being pushed back by the Messerschmitt escorts. The British pilots stuck to their task and two Polish pilots in 501 Squadron shot down a Messerschmitt each. One of the fallen pilots was the author of the confident letter from Chapter 1, Hans-Otto Lessing. Shortly after, a pilot from 32 Squadron registered another kill. Nevertheless, the bombers continued onward, skirting anti-aircraft gunfire intermittently. The odds seemed to be in favour of the Luftwaffe, but, significantly, cloud was building up over both Hornchurch and North Weald.

Ultimately, the attacks were aborted because of bad weather and the Germans were punished by the chasing RAF fighters. Thus, both raids were an unmitigated disaster. As the planes turned for home, they were harried by the RAF, specifically those of 46, 85, 151, 256 Squadrons. To a man, these pilots were buoyed by the sight of all these German planes of abandoning their raids. So too were onlookers on the ground below and the following day's newspaper articles were exultant. It truly seemed that the Spitfires and Hurricanes had scared the Germans off. Richard Milne was one of the first to attack; as he chased down one bomber, the plane's rear gun was firing inaccurately at him, but Milne's bullets were hitting the German plane, which subsequently crashed, killing all 6 men on board. In retaliation, two planes from 151 Squadron were shot down.

Squadron Leader Peter Townsend led his 85 Squadron after the bombers, but his attempts were blocked by the German fighter escorts. Another confrontation ensued, and this was now the general pattern in different pockets of the sky as the bombers headed east, where they dropped bombs on air base a railway station. Townsend, incidentally, went on to have a secret love affair with a Royal after the war as he became entwined with Princess Margaret. There had been rumours that they were involved, and the media exploded with conjecture when a photographer caught the Princess pick fluff off his uniform, which was an intimate gesture. Unfortunately, as a divorced man, the Church of England and Queen Elizabeth II made their marriage impossible, though recently unearthed documents, as reported in numerous newspapers, suggest that perhaps the young Royal simply lost interest in the Battle of Britain hero.

The RAF were chasing them all the way, and the worsening weather made it difficult for the escorts to cover the retreat of the bombers. Joachim Koepsell was almost flanked by a Hurricane hidden in the clouds, as detailed in Price's *Hardest Day*. He only became aware of its presence at the last moment, but his wealth of flying experience told as he forced his plane into a hard dive. He knew that if the Hurricane followed him, which it did, its engine would cut out. Therefore, Koepsell was able to return to base unharmed., while one by one, the British pilots ran out of ammunition and were forced to turn back to base.

By the end of these encounters, 32 bombs had been deposited over the town of Shoeburyness, and there were fatalities. 1 bomb exploded on an air-raid shelter in a garden, killing the couple inside. The bomb that landed on the railway station killed a signalman. Regarding the physical destruction, 2 houses were completely destroyed, while 20 more seriously damaged. The nearby gunnery range was also hit, but with little damaged incurred. Over 200 bombs were dropped on Shoeburyness' mud flats and sand banks. They had delayed fuses, and many went off at random intervals in the hours after the departure of the German bombers. In Deal, another small town, 24 bombs were dropped. Luckily, nobody died in the attack, but several houses and buildings were left in various states of damage, including the evacuated Royal infirmary.

One major consequence of the battle was Hermann Goering's belief that in future engagements, escort planes had to stick even closer to the bombers. For pilots like Hans Schmoller, this new directive blunted the effectiveness of fighters – instead of having the freedom to use speed and altitude to their advantage, they were forced to stick to a specific zone in the sky, handing the enemy the initiative.

The day ended with 69 destroyed Luftwaffe aircraft and 27 damaged planes returned to France. 94 German aircrew were killed, 25 were wounded and forty were taken prisoner. 31 British planes were destroyed, 11 pilots died and 19 were wounded. British losses on the ground amounted to 51 military personnel and 13 civilians. Of the 165 British planes ordered into the skies, only 103 were able to find the enemy. Only 3 planes from 46 Squadron intercepted the enemy, which was a poor return and a missed opportunity as they did not have the chance to turn their cannons on the German bombers and fighters.

Both sides reported great wins – the British proudly reported it had 140 kills, and the Germans said they had 147. The Nazis claimed victory, but they had been terribly surprised by the stiffness of the British defence. Certainly, the pilots earned their beer that night, but there would not be much time to rest – there was always a new day and the risk of another Luftwaffe attack. All in all, it was the Luftwaffe who felt more keenly the setbacks of August 18th, The Hardest Day.

CHAPTER 4:
The Media Reaction

Winston Churchill once quipped that history was going to be kind to him, especially since he was going to write it. There are scores of other quotes about writing history, most of which deal with the idea that historical writing is nothing more than a way to create a fable, a skewed story that everybody can agree on. Its power lies not in its truth, but in its ability to bond people together under the banner of a 'nation' or an idea.

When Goethe said, 'writing history is a method of getting rid of the past', he could not have been speaking about the British, whose modern sensibilities and neuroses are informed deeply, for good and for bad, by their wartime experience, of which the Battle of Britain is a fundamental part. After The Hardest Day, it was obvious for contemporary newspapers that something historic was occurring, one with profound implications for the world. Reporting in 1940 also provided a great opportunity for some morale boosting propaganda. We can also take a look at modern commemorations of August 18th, which reveal that the trauma of being under German attack is still vividly remembered, even if many of the protagonists lived humbly in the shadows.

Media Reaction In 1940: The Hardest Day & The Battle of Britain

On August 19th, one day after The Hardest Day, newspapers were crowing about the number of German planes shot down. *The Times* reported that hundreds of Luftwaffe machines had been destroyed. All of the papers based their reports on information provided by the British government, which also spoke of the 22 British fighters that had been lost, and of the 12 shot-down pilots who were known to be safe.

The general idea which ran across these stories is correct – August 18th was a day of heavy losses for both sides, with the Germans coming out the worst of it. But the reported numbers were slightly inflated in order to spin a particular story. Alfred Price ably demonstrates in his book that the number of 22 destroyed British fighters could not possibly tally with reality as this figure did not take into account planes that been shot up while still on the ground or the planes that had been abandoned in the air.

In communiques to the German press, the Nazi government followed the same instinct as their British counterparts, with the number of enemy losses given a positive glean. Thus, journalists in Nazi Germany reported that scores of British planes had been shot down and that 33 barrage balloons had been destroyed. There is a reference to a British plane being brought down by flak, which apparently happened on the

French coast on the night of the 18th, but this is not corroborated by British reports.

Both the British and Germans used the euphemism 'failed to return home', which allowed official reports to avoid having to come out and directly say how many of their planes had been shot down. Using this vague term, planes that reached enemy territory, even if they had crash landed, were not recorded as losses. In fact, both the Nazi and British air forces reported such inflated figures, propogandists on either side of the English Channel felt no need to doctor the numbers further before they hit the press.

George Orwell said that language can corrupt thought, while Price quoted Dean Acheson, an American stateman and lawyer, when he said that propaganda was a type of lying which 'consists in nearly deceiving your friends, without quite deceiving your enemies'. If the RAF and the Luftwaffe were battling to control the skies in August of 1940, their respective papers were locked in a battle to control the narrative, hoping to convince their public that their side was winning the war.

Aside from the 18th, the media covered other red-letter days in the summer of 1940.

On August 27th, *The Guardian* reported that the air-raid alarms went off at 12:40 am. The RAF were bombing factories in Berlin, in an operation hampered by poor weather. This is a little-known part of the Battle of Britain – many people are not aware the British planes went on bombing raids of their own while England was under threat of Nazi invasion, and the misconception is that these raids happened later in World War II. Nevertheless, these pilots never enjoyed the same appreciation as Churchill's Few; the area bombing tactic of the RAF when over German soil has long been controversial.

These attacks followed other raids on aerodromes in Holland, France and Belgium. In Norway, the RAF attacked moored flying boats. While Berlin was being bombed, Leipzig was also attacked, and *The Guardian* crowed about how the normally unflappable Germans were forced into air-raid shelters.

What is interesting about this story is that it is a pretty accurate retelling of what happened, but this side of the war, as previously mentioned, is not as well-known. The Hardest Day is a date with more of a historical cache, but the media reports were less reliable.

The reporting on September 16th, the day after Battle of Britain Day, was more or less faithful to the truth, even though the number of RAF kills on this date, with propaganda in mind, were exaggerated.

The article in *The Guardian* was full of eyewitness accounts because the action took place over London. The newspaper reported on the crowds of people who cheered when a gaggle of Spitfires took down a German bomber over a London neighbourhood. One Luftwaffe pilot who was forced to bale out over the city had to watch as the locals tore his parachute into strips for souvenirs. A British pilot, who was also forced to eject from his plane, landed in a back garden, and when he met the garden's owner, he exclaimed: 'I managed to get him before they got me'.

Battle of Britain Day will be examined further in the conclusion of this book, but at this juncture, we can see that were some differences how August 18th and September 15th were reported. The Hardest Day came at time when the Luftwaffe was in a slightly stronger position, so the media were used to inflate any British successes. By mid-September, the RAF were in the ascendant, and media reports could freely publish first-hand accounts from ordinary Londoners who delighted in every German loss. These heroic young men impressed everyone, and the fighting in the sky made for great propaganda. Yet, normal life was maintained below, and reports abound of normal people looking up to see dogfights above them before going back to an everyday activity like a tennis match or filling a bath. In nearby, neutral Ireland, a 5-page editorial in the *Irish Times* evaluated the Battle of Britain and asked the key question – 'how long can the Luftwaffe continue to lose machines… how long can it stand the loss of so many trained men?'.

The Modern World Remembers

It is not an exaggeration to say that our way of life has been made possible by the Allies winning the Second World War. As such, it is no surprise that this debt is commemorated every year. In 2015, on the 75th anniversary of The Hardest Day, the celebrations were bigger than ever.

The *Bexley Times* reported from Biggin Hill. To mark the occasion, 18 Spitfires and 6 Hurricanes flew in various formations in the sky overhead, ably assisted by reenactors on the ground dressed in World War II costume. The airport's Head of Communications, Simon Ames, spoke of wanting to honour the work of all the heroes who endured the constant threat of Nazi attack. This included pilots, engineers, armourers, operations staff and ground crews. These men and women, to paraphrase Winston Churchill, were responsible for turning Germany's supposed week of domination into a week of British victory.

The newspaper also features the comment of Robin Brooks, an aviation historian who helps run the Biggin Hill Heritage Hangar. He described the skies on August 18th as 'hell in the air'. Another aviation historian, Anthony Moor, is quoted as saying that the attacks on this day were the consequence of the Luftwaffe's arrogant and fatally flawed belief that the RAF was on its last legs. Undoubtedly, the pilots were exhausted and stretched, but they could draw on hidden reserves of energy and strength to keep flying against the Luftwaffe.

The report does contain, in the midst of all the tributes, a surprising anecdote, one which was briefly touched upon in Chapter 1. A Dornier bomber flew low close to the air base after sustaining heavy fire from British fighters. The pilot of the German plane probably did not count on being fired upon from the Home Guard and their assortment of rifles. The plane burst into flames and crashed, in what was a definite high point for the much-maligned Home Guard, which was comprised of men who were too young or too old to fight. In later years, they would also be known as Dad's Army, a term popularized by a TV show of the same name.

The BBC also witnessed the Spitfires and Hurricanes take flight to commemorate the fabled Few who intercepted multiple German attacks in 1940. According to reporter Clark Ainsworth, the crowd of 3,000 people, a mixture of civilians and veterans, gasped as these vintage planes lit up the sky with their prestige and acrobatic maneuvres. Apparently, the planes were still a pleasure to fly, which shows how much these events can offer hands-on history and a practical demonstration of how both the Spitfire and the Hurricane helped win the Battle of Britain. And anyone who has seen TV presenter Alain de Cadenent be surprised by the thunderous roar of a Spitfire as it flies just above his head – which appears as an outtake on an American documentary of the 60th anniversary of the Spitfire – will know that the machine comes with a lot of power.

The presence of Barbara Miller, working for Australia's ABC News, is proof that that many of the pilots who flew in the long summer of 1940 were from different corners of the globe, and the repelling of the Luftwaffe was a symbolic act of great evil, which still grabs international interest today. She interviewed Tony Pickering, who, as a callow 20-year-old, flew in the Battle of Britain. He remembered those 'exciting times'; days where he could only concentrate on doing his job and hope for the best. Flypast organiser Colin Hitchin commented on how when the pilots took off, they never knew if the base would still be standing on their return. He added that men like Pickering were hanging on 'by the skin of their teeth'. Now, many years later, Pickering was a feted guest in a national celebration. As reported in *Express*, he reminisced on experiences of 1940: 'I don't think I was ever afraid. I was enthusiastic but I had to make sure I wasn't too enthusiastic. I couldn't take on the German air force myself, we were a team. But I was too young to be fearful. We knew something was up – we had a job to do and we did it'.

Unfortunately, the 80th anniversary, which was scheduled to be celebrated in 2020, may be cancelled or significantly rolled back on account of the global COVID-19 lockdown.

Written By The Winners

2015 was also the 70th anniversary of the liberation of Auschwitz. Both The Hardest Day and the Holocaust are still commemorated, and both have their own poignant significance. Writing for *The Tech*, Suri Bandler argues that commemorations are vital for making a better world: 'It is by doing *projects* in memory of such tragedies that will help us develop a society that is conscious of what is at stake when some do not respect the rights of others to exist... we can never allow the past to be laid to rest'.

The Battle of Britain is more complex than it is sometimes presented, and today, there are some politicians who still mine the Battle of Britain for propaganda. But if Epifanio de los Santos was correct in saying that 'writing history is writing the soul of the past', then it is good and right that people since the end of the World War II, from newspapers in 1940 to modern commemorations, have honoured the events and protagonists of August 18th. There are many passionate historians and curators who lovingly tend to the legacy of different airfields and radar stations, and to the legacy of the real pilots and WAAF plotters who focused on doing their job in difficult circumstances, and who after the war, lived quiet lives as unassuming heroes.

CHAPTER 5:
The Importance of Radar

Hermann Goering never fully grasped how the British successfully used radar to repel his Luftwaffe on The Hardest Day, even though he knew that disabling this radar network could give an advantage to the German air attacks. Yet, even though he became exasperated by their failure to successfully achieve this, he still switched tactics in September of 1940, effectively marking the end of the Battle of Britain, when he ordered his planes to bomb British cities instead of airfields and radar stations. This terrible new phase of the air war was known as the Blitz.

The symbolism of the Blitz and is known around the world. It is a touchstone for a certain kind of 'Bulldog spirit', of defiance as air raid sirens pierced the sky. The onset of this new phase of the air war over England is evidence of that the Nazis knew they had lost the Battle of Britain and had failed on August 18th. It was a sign, also, that Goering, and his

Luftwaffe, did not really understand the reason for this failure.

The Chain Home and Dowding Systems

The British radar network was the Chain Home System. Its functional name belies the staggering fact that this early-warning system was the first of its kind, and the first military radar system to become fully operational, which happened when the last station was completed in 1938. The Dowding System, comprised of stations like Biggin Hill and Kenley, and it was staffed by WAAF plotters. The WAAF sent information gleaned from their screens to the central HQ, where it was interpreted and relayed to regional stations and the pilots, which was another world first. Crucially, as has already been discussed, these stations were in constant contact via a huge network of underground telephone cables.

The Dowding System, named after Air Chief Marshal Sir Hugh Dowding, divided the UK into 4 groups, numbered 10-13. 10 Group covered South West England and Wales; 11 Group was responsible for London and the South East; 12 Group covered the Midlands, East Anglia and some of northern England; 13 Group, finally, was tasked with observing parts of the English north, Scotland, and Northern Ireland. Over the course of the Battle of Britain, 11 Group was unquestionably the busiest sector. Dowding's 4 group commanders were Air Vice-Marshals Keith Park, who helped bury the infamous Red Baron in 1918; Christopher Quintin Brand; Trafford Leigh-Mallory; and Richard Saul.

Hugh Dowding was a well-respected man, and faith in his intelligence and technical knowledge was unwavering. Nevertheless, his obdurate personality blocked his career and his superiors wanted to retire him by 1940, but with the increasing threat of German air battles, his was asked to stay on until the danger had passed. His eventual retirement stung his colleagues – they were sorry to see the back of such a capable man. Many pilots, however, never came in close contact with him. He struck up a fruitful partnership with Park, whose strategic brain improved the functionality of Dowding's ideas. Like Dowding, Park was task-orientated and, despite his sternness, was beloved as a man of great integrity. Park had the common touch that, perhaps, Dowding lacked. He was a great team leader and he used humour to put his men at ease. What is more, he seemed to genuinely care about the welfare of his pilots, which cannot be said of every leader. Once, he milled around an air bases unrecognized, hoping to get a feel for what his men were experiencing.

Radar allowed great flexibility in RAF's tactics. Air Vice-Marshall Richard Saul was a proponent of hitting the enemy early and shooting down as many as possible. Park preferred to be more judicious, intercepting only what was necessary in order to ensure the RAF's survival. Using the Chain Home system, he could decide how many British planes would fly to meet the enemy, and when. It was all designed around ideas of maximizing efficiency and avoiding getting attacked while British planes were grounded or being refueled. Park's preference also meant his smaller attack units were fast, could work independently, and were harder targets to hit. In addition, the use of fewer planes made suffering a major defeat in the air impossible, and it allowed plotters to try and place RAF in a position where they could emerge unsighted with the sun behind them.

It was a demanding job for the plotters, and they had to sound confident at all times, even when the unfolding action was unclear. If they gave the wrong order, it was imperative to wait a moment before correcting it. Giving conflicting orders one after another was dangerous.

The Chain Home system had to be modified when the RAF realized that planes flying at a low altitude could not be detected, so a Chain Home Low network was put into operation. Its rotating radio beam, unliked the fixed beam of the original system, could not detect height. Rather, it could detect planes at 500 feet at ranges up to 100 miles away. Clearly, the system had become quite sophisticated considering that the idea for it had been born in the hysterical fear that the Germans had developed a radio wave inspired 'death ray' in the 1930s. The fear was allayed by the quick realization that radio could not be used as weapon, but rather as a way to detect incoming aircraft. A quick test with a BBC transmitter and a RAF plane proved their theory and set in motion a chain of events that ultimately culminated with the Chain Home and Dowding systems working in unison during on The Hardest Day and beyond.

Nevertheless, according to the RAF Museum, the system did have some flaws. Owing to the fact that they faced out to sea, which made sighting German planes flying in British skies a little bit harder. Thus, an Observer Corps had to watch the skies, track the enemy incursion, and determine how many planes were flying and their altitude. In addition, it took the Luftwaffe only 20 minutes to reach Croydon after crossing the Channel, and it took between 6 and 16 minutes to process all the information and get pilots in the sky.

Anthony Cumming's *Did Radar Win The Battle of Britain* raises the idea that radar was not that effective. This account argues that a certain myth has grown up around the long summer of 1940 – a myth that is now a fundamental part of British identity. Wing Commander H. R. Allen was a frequent critic of the how the RAF was responding to the attacks, and his personal opinion was that early warning system was only reliable 50% of the time. He preferred to put his trust in the Observer Corps. Unfortunately, in inclement or cloudy weather, their effectiveness was limited. Added to this, was the fact that plotters might not be able to precisely locate enemy aircraft and even experienced British pilots struggled to identify where the Germans were if they were given the wrong vector to locate them. In essence, every link in this chain had to be highly trained, but achieving this in wartime scenario was exceedingly difficult, resulting in mechanics and operators having little practical knowledge of how to fulfil their roles.

Despite these serious limitations, Winston Churchill was moved to write in 1949 that this dual system of radar and human observers was the main source of information about incoming planes and vital in winning the Battle of Britain. Taking into account abstract qualities like 'grit' and 'spirit', the emotion that stems from defending a homeland and the quality of Hurricanes and Spitfires, it seems like Churchill was correct in his appraisal. Quite simply, the use of radar was a potent tool in the Battle of Britain, especially on August 18th, when Goering threw the full weight of his Luftwaffe against the British defenses.

But any war is defined by the ebb and flow of victory, and when the Germans invented their own radar system, it swung the tide of World War II decidedly in favour of the Nazis. It would take a near-suicidal mission to wrestle the initiative back into British hands.

Operation Biting

By 1942, a little while after the events of this book, there were no British troops left on the European mainland and the British Government were now forced had resorted to attacking Nazi-controlled Europe from the air.

Despite initial Allied successes, the Germans started becoming remarkably successful in shooting down Allied planes, and the British started to suspect that the Nazis had developed a superior radar system, which allowed them to easily identify and destroy enemy aircraft easily. These suspicions were confirmed when RAF reconnaissance discovered that the Nazis had built a radar station on the French coast, complete with new radar equipment. The objective now was to capture this new radar system and analyze it. This daring mission was codenamed Operation Biting.

Located in the cliffs near the town of Bruneval, the Germans in this station had two advantages: the Freya-Meldung-Freya and the Würzburg system. The Freya specialized in detection, while the Würzburg tracked planes and calculated artillery fire, making planes easier to hit. The British wanted to capture the Würzburg so that they could develop effective countermeasures against it.

Obtaining the Würzburg would be dangerous. A frontal assault on the cliffside fortifications would have been suicidal, so the plan was to drop British commandos behind enemy lines. These men, after a completing their objectives, could then escape from the beach by speedboat. The stakes were incredibly high, with the battle to dominate the sky in the balance. Furthermore, Britain had never used paratroopers before, so this would be a baptism of fire for the freshly trained men.

The Brigade was divided into five sections, all named after British heroes. There was *Nelson*, *Hardy*, *Jellicoe*, *Drake* and *Rodney*. Jellico, Hardy and Drake were tasked with assaulting the main radar station and a nearby chateau where German soldiers were quartered. Nelson would attack the coastal defenses, which was important for making a successful escape possible. Finally, Rodney defended the rear in order to block any German counterattack.

Operation Biting was planned for the end of February 1942. The troops, who were later dubbed the Red Devils on account of their red berets, would be mission-ready by then, and their incursion into Nazi territory would be helped by a high moon and a low tide.

After flying through heavy flak, the paratroopers landed on the night of February 27th. One section, Rodney, missed the drop zone by two miles, and the radios did not work. Out of necessity, runners were used for communication between different sections, but it was far from ideal.

The mission was now underway. In the chateau, a solitary German was killed as he shot at the paratroopers from the Jellico, Hardy and Drake sections. Another two Germans were captured; under interrogation, the pair revealed that most of the German soldiers had been moved inland. Meanwhile, the

Nelson section was engaged in heavy firefights with Germans on the coast.

The Würzburg, and a German technician, was then captured by Jellico, Hardy and Drake. The paratroopers had to dismantle the Würzburg, but this was a race against time as German reinforcements were on the way approaching their position. The British soldiers used brute force to pull apart key components of the system, before bringing them to the beach under heavy fire.

There, they continued to be attacked, this time by a hidden machine gun. By this time, the chateau had also been recaptured by the Nazis, and they were firing at the British men from the rear. Jellico, Hardy and Drake attacked the chateau and defeated the Germans once more. After returning to the beach, they found that the machine gun nest had been neutralized by Rodney section, which had fought its way back to the rendezvous.

The paratroopers were now stuck on the beach. Flashing lights from the road indicated that a fresh German attack was on the way. The British soldiers could not contact their boats by radio. In a desperate attempt to signal their position, the British fired flares into the night sky, illuminating for friend and foe to see. After a few minutes of panicked waiting, rescue boats finally reached the beach. Under covering fire from these boats, the men entered the vessels with pieces of the Würzburg and German prisoners. In the chaos, some of the boats were overcrowded while others were half-empty. Escorted by Spitfires, the paratroopers made it home safely the following morning.

The success of Operation Biting lifted British morale considerably. Furthermore, the British were successfully able to counteract the new German technology, which handed the Allies an advantage in the air. After the raid, the Germans increased their defenses around the radar station in Bruneval, which made it easier to target during the D-Day landings. This daring mission was an important moment and a major turning point in World War II, and it helped demonstrate that the Nazi war machine could be defeated.

Operation Biting also betrays a German oversight in the Battle of Britain. British radar stations were small, hard to hit targets. If the Germans had launched an audacious raid of their own on a British station, they could have destroyed a mast and affected a serious delay in Britain's radar system. In response, the British could have then defended the stations with heavy defenses, which, as shown in the case of Bruneval, would have presented a bigger target from the air. The Germans did not try any of this, and so British radar stations were relatively untroubled during the summer of 1940.

The Battle of the Beams: From Biggin to Biting

The Second World War began on September 1, 1939 and ended on September 2, 1945. In this timespan, a bitter conflict was fought in Europe, Africa, and Asia, one marked by many burning questions. During the Battle of Britain, people wondered if Hitler was coming, while freedom-loving people trapped on the European continent, and an under-pressure Joseph Stalin, wondered when an Allied invasion would land on French beaches. In finest hours and the darkest ones, not much could seem certain in a world locked in an existential struggle between good and evil. Eventually, the combined power of Churchill, Stalin, and Roosevelt made German capitulation inevitable.

But if one thing was constant, it was that the side with the best radar held an advantage.

Looking back at The Hardest Day, we can acknowledge that this fateful date was not just about ferocious dogfights and acts of personal valour. As the order to 'scramble' was relayed through the Chain Home and Dowding systems in response to the three attacks, it is undeniable that the British use of radar helped them win the Battle of Britain and, ultimately, the Second World War itself.

CHAPTER 6:
British & Foreign Pilots, Women on the Ground

Who were the pilots defending England from the threat of German invasion? For many on the ground, both on August 18th and during the entirety of the Battle of Britain, the pilots whizzed by in a blur, and ordinary civilians either ran for cover or went about their day nonplussed. Then the threat of German invasion passed, and the men became rightly lionized as 'the Few', but their passing into legend tells us precious little about the people who defended England so stoutly.

This chapter is about the British and foreign pilots who defended British skies. Of the foreign contingent, there were the Irish pilots, like John Hemingway, who was shot down by the Germans, and John Finucane, the youngest Wing Commander in RAF history and the man dubbed 'the fighting Gael' by the *New York Times* on account of the shamrock he had painted under his wing. There were also pilots from the Commonwealth and the USA; Jewish pilots; and Czechs and Poles, men who were forced from their homeland by the seemingly unstoppable Nazi war machine and its brand of Fascist racism. In all their flights, they were supported by aircrews on the ground, and by innumerable women in air bases.

If the legacy of defeating Nazism in 1945 underpinned the foundation of the United Nations, then the Battle of Britain was this concept in a microcosm: a multinational cast of men and women from different backgrounds coming together for the greater good, to safeguard the values of democracy and liberty in the world.

Bruce Hancock & Robert Doe

Sgt Pilot Bruce Hancock lost his life on August 18th, aged 26. He was a volunteer reservist who, in the middle of intense battle of The Hardest Day, took to the air in unarmed training plane. Unfortunately for Hancock, this flight was doomed from the moment a German spotted him and turned all of its guns on him. With no guns and facing a bigger plane, the young Englishman flew straight into the enemy, using his own aircraft as a weapon. Hancock sacrificed his life and the entire crew of the bomber was also lost. These men, German and English, were the last to die on August 18th.

According to his nephew, who was born three years after Hancock died, in an interview with the *Oxford Mail*, the pilot boasted in the pub that if he saw a German plane in the sky, he would ram it. On The Hardest Day, he made good on his boast and paid with his life, proving that his actions against the bomber were a product of some deeply-held conviction that the Germans should be stopped by any means necessary, rather than a spur of the moment act of desperation. Though the RAF had a culture of maintaining a stiff upper lip, so perhaps his bravado was a public way of demonstrating he was unaffected by nerves, even though most pilots did feel a real sense of fear. Or perhaps it was genuine confidence. In a letter to his mother, another pilot, Lieutenant Ronald Wright, claimed that morale so high, even one British plane could defeat the entire arsenal of the Luftwaffe.

In 2015, at a ceremony to commemorate one of the fiercest days of fighting in the Battle of Britain, a plaque to Hancock was re-dedicated and a new one was put in place to celebrate the role of Windrush airfield. Finally, this unsung hero in the efforts to repel the Nazi invasion finally got his due reward and recognition.

Stephen Bungay's book, *The Most Dangerous Enemy*, is bookended by stories about Robert Doe. A sickly child, this fighter pilot held a deep-held conviction that he was going to die during the Battle of Britain. By his own admission, he was not a very good student and he passed the examination to become a pilot by a mere 1%. Doe had spent sad, lonely childhood shooting the heads off flowers, and as it turns out, his finely-honed air rifle skills turned him into something of an ace. On his very first mission, he destroyed two enemy planes.

In the RAF, however, aces were not really celebrated. The number of kills achieved by an individual pilot was valued more highly by the Luftwaffe. German pilots saw themselves as knights, and medals were awarded in direct relation to the number of confirmed kills. Arguably, this promoted a culture of recklessness that got many German pilots killed.

When a 1985 Channel 4 documentary profiled Doe and his role in the Battle of Britain, a road sweeper came up to thank him, and people started calling him 'sir'. The reaction he got brought tears to his eyes. He published his memoirs in 1991. Bungay praises him as a gentle man, one who deserved greater recognition in his life.

New Zealanders

July saw the Battle of Britain in its earliest phase – before the concerted attacks of August and The Hardest Day, the Luftwaffe were busying themselves with sporadic raids on British targets. Even at this stage, airmen from New Zealand were involved in the fight. A Spitfire squadron led by Officer Carbury destroyed a German bomber over Scotland. On July 9, Lieutenant Deere was in a Spitfire near Dover, and his was involved in near head-on collision with a German fighter while his squadron was trying to take out a reconnaissance plane. He crash-landed into a field and, while being almost being blinded by the smoke and oil, forced his way out of the plane. He was back in action the very next day.

The RAF and its Antipodean contingent were scoring successes for most of July, but a change in German tactics forced the British to adapt its tactics. On July 24th, a force of 50 German aircraft – a mixture of bombers and escorting fighters – attacked the Thames Estuary. 54 Squadron, led by Deere, shot down 5 planes, with 2 of those crashing onto the streets below. This pattern was maintained until August. As we already know, German planes started to target radar stations, airfields, and factories in an intense phase of the Battle of Britain, one which encompassed The Hardest Day.

In this period, New Zealand pilots were kept active. 213 Squadron, led by a Kiwi by the name if McGregor, stopped a bombing raid in its tracks, downing 7 enemy planes in the process. The rest of the bombers were forced to drop bombs far from their intended targets. In another dramatic episode, a force of 20 bombers made for Kent. Deere led the defence and downed an enemy plane, while another New Zealander chased a Messerschmitt as far as the French coast. Later that same day, Deere bagged another two kills, and he once again forced the Luftwaffe to drop their bombs harmlessly in open fields rather than on a radar station or airfield. On the same day, Officer W. S. Williams crash-landed his Spitfire, which blew up just after the New Zealander exited the plane. Williams was killed a few months later in October.

Deere also chased a Messerschmitt to Calais in another dogfight. After shooting his quarry down, he was attacked by 5 German fighters. He managed to evade them, but he was forced to bale out of his bullet-ridden Spitfire. He later described vividly his escape from the plane, which was veering in all directions before he felt the reassuring tug of his parachute. Luckily, a bush broke his fall.

In all of these engagements, a squadron had to climb quickly into the sky to gain an advantage, which would be supplemented by knowledge from plotters in the Operation Room. Aside from that, the air battles became an individual battle of wills between opposing pilots. On The Hardest Day, one New Zealander commented on how from their height, they could swoop in on the Germans below and destroy their plane, especially if they ran into them unexpectedly. Another remembered how an interception of German squadron resulted in his shooting down of a Messerschmitt, whose smoky tailspin ended by crashing into sea. Another Kiwi on August 18th reported that he attacked a Messerschmitt but was forced to break off the attack because he was being chased by another German fighter. The pilot turned and got a shot off at his pursuer, but now he was being tailed by three Germans. While he engaged in evasive maneuvres, he managed to down one bomber, attack another, and then make it safely home after running out of ammunition.

By the end of the Battle of Britain, 95 New Zealand pilots fought with dedication and heroism, and with no little success, against wave after wave of Luftwaffe attacks. By helping to keep the Nazis at bay, an important blow was stuck against Hitler's plan to dominate Europe.

Sergeant Joan Mortimer and Flight Officer Elspeth Henderson

At the onset of World War II, the Women's Auxiliary Airforce (WAAF) was created. Although women were forbidden to fly in combat – some civilian planes were handled by female pilots – the staff of the WAAF played a fundamental role in The Hardest Day, all the while exposed to a myriad of dangers. Their responsibilities included packing parachuting, crewing barrage balloons, performing radar and plane maintenance, working with reconnaissance photos and intelligence reports, and crucially, plotting the movement of British and German planes during the Battle of Britain.

Joan Mortimer and Elspeth Henderson were two female officers in the WAAF, and both survived the attacks on

Biggins Hill, showing great courage under German bombs. Mortimer was manning the switchboard at Biggin during the Luftwaffe bombardment. Despite orders to abandon her post, she stayed and passed on telephone messages to her superiors. She was still sitting there when all of Biggins' anti-craft gunners were destroyed and the gunners killed.

Her bravery did not end there. Once the all clear was given, she rushed outside with red flags so she could mark for the RAF the location of all the unexploded bombs. While doing this, one unexploded bomb went off and sent her flying, tearing her clothes and winding her in the process. Her bravery came at the cost of her hearing, and she was eventually discharged in 1941. Sadly, her fiancé, a pilot, was shot down a few months after the Biggin raid.

Mortimer, affectionately known as Elizabeth, was awarded the Military Medal for her heroic conduct, which was uncommon for the time as she was a woman, and she was later honoured with having a road named after her in 2010 and with a write-up in the local paper, the *East Anglian Daily Times*.

Henderson, for her part, wound up at Biggin after only 2 weeks of training to be a plotter. According to a feature in the *Daily Record*, she was driven by an intense belief that everyone should do their part, and that it was immoral to sit at home and do nothing while the men were fighting on the front. Aside from her strong convictions, her obvious talent saw her rise to the rank of corporal, which placed many other WAAF officers under her command.

She survived the devastating raids of August 18th, but she had to live and work through numerous German bombing raids.

In one, an air raid shelter was hit, killing most of the WAAF women inside. Henderson was one of the first to dig them out. A subsequent raid saw her Operations room hit directly, but the corporal stayed at her post until the very last moment – leading by example and commanding her staff to keep working – then escaped through a window, dodging wild flames and falling bombs.

For all other bravery, she too was awarded the Military Medal. Owing to her natural shyness, she did not tell her parents about the raids on the 18th and through August because she did not want to worry them, nor did she mention her medal citation. She did, however, note that the roof of the Operations room was flimsy and not bomb-proof. The news of the award only came to light when reporters came calling to her door. Even though she kept the pilots flying, she rarely spoke about her wartime experiences.

The Few and the Forgotten

The internet is a reservoir of knowledge, but a search for information on these brave pilots does not yield a lot of interesting results about that fateful summer in 1940. Sadly, obituary after obituary pops up, commemorating a generation that witnessed so much as it slips into the next world. This is the inevitable march of time, and it applies to every dimension of World War II. For example, the 75th anniversary of the D-Day landings in 2019 was charged with an added poignancy because many realized that most of the soldiers that stormed French beaches were no longer alive, and that their presence at these kinds of events would dwindle to zero.

We already know that many of these pilots found it difficult to move on after the war. What we might call Post-Traumatic

Stress Disorder afflicted some; the sound of a ringing phone, for instance, could bring up frightful memories for years after the Battle of Britain. For others, post-war xenophobia impacted them. The Poles, who hated the drizzly weather and the food, who charmed the local women endlessly, who downed a large number of German planes, were left stranded after victory was declared in Europe. Stalin's Russia were the new conquers of Poland and the East. Naturally, many of the Poles wanted to remain in England, but they were suddenly unwelcome. Graffiti that could have come straight out of modern-day Brexit Britain was daubed on walls and they were told England was for the English. The *Daily Mail* – a paper not known for its enlightened views on immigration – wrestled over how these Polish fighters could be so 'humiliated' by 'an ungrateful nation'.

During the war, there was some distrust of foreign pilots because they did not speak English, which had the knock-on effect of making these pilots have less flying discipline, and the Controllers felt that they – the Czechs in particular – chatted too much on the radio.

Hard-Fought Victories

The Hardest Day and the Battle of Britain's success was secured through the use of powerful radar, faulty German tactics, through the voice of Churchill and because of the sophistication of Hurricanes and Spitfires. And, also, in the actions of these pilots, British and foreign, supported by the brave WAAF, who ran to their planes when they heard the shout, 'scramble!'. They took off not knowing if they would ever make it back safely, delivering Britain's finest hour as they measured their lives in minutes.

These were the ordinary people who gave everything to extract a hard-fought victory from the hardest of days in the Battle of Britain.

Conclusion – The Tide Turns

Once the dust had settled after this long day, there was much to consider.

One of the biggest casualties of The Hardest Day was the Stuka bomber, which was pulled out of service; this infamous plane was too slow, could not defend itself, and needed to operate where it had air superiority, which it clearly did not have in the Battle of Britain. They would also be needed at a later date, if the planned of invasion of Britain was ever going to take place.

The events of the 18th also forced the Germans into changing how they deployed their planes. Even though their pilots had flown around 1,500 sorties on this day, there was not much to show for it. The RAF were successful in intercepting incoming planes and the Luftwaffe rarely caught them by surprise. In addition, airfields in any war are quite difficult to destroy, particularly if they are rudimentary and made of grass. Despite the bombardments of Eagle Week, British airfields were not seriously disrupted. Furthermore, the 18th was a day of attritional battle, and if the RAF was to be destroyed, then the Luftwaffe would also be wrecked in the process.

Apart from the excellent used of radar, The Hardest Day saw many RAF sorties attack German reconnaissance planes, which may seem curious, but it contributed to the Luftwaffe's fatal lack of information, which included not knowing how many British planes were on hand to defend against a raid. Guns firing from the ground also destroyed a handful of German planes, catching them as they flew low. However, these guns also hit their own RAF planes. In addition, because German targets were purely military, civilian loss of life was low. Overall, loss of life in the Battle of Britain was minimal, with 5,000 fallen military personnel in total. Bungay drew on his inner Churchill when he wrote that 'never has so crucial a battle been won at so low a cost in life'. The Germans ran a greater risk of losing life because their bombers needed a large crew. A downed bomber cost multiple lives while a destroyed fighter usually only cost the life of one man.

At this stage of the war, British production was far outstripping Germany's, a fact which pleased Churchill. The Prime Minister foresaw the RAF achieving superiority in the air the longer the conflict went on. He needed men to fly those planes, and on August 20th, he celebrated them in a speech in the Commons: 'Never in the field of human conflict was so much owed by many to so few'. The Luftwaffe frequently cast themselves as knights of the sky, and now Churchill was making the same allusions, as his words rang with a Shakespearean air. Throughout the war, ordinary British people listening to his speeches noted the Elizabethan air of his sentiments.

According to Bungay's book, reaction from the pilots to being referred to in this manner was varied. Robert Doe, who pops up throughout the book, was taken aback by the acclaim and felt, for the first time, like he had done something of note in his life. Others met it with sardonic wit – *of course we're the few, we've lost so many men!* It was probably the first time they stopped to think about the overriding significance of the battle. These were young men who chased beer and women, who saw war as a sport. They focused solely on doing their job and following orders, so hearing these gilded words probably came as a shock.

They were being hailed for their bravery, but these were also skilled men. Civilians on the ground could not fully appreciate the skill these men had had to utilize on The Hardest Day. Aside from deflection shooting (described in the Introduction), RAF pilots had to learn how to 'bounce', which meant emerging from the sun, shooting off a few rounds for a few seconds, before slipping back into the sun, avoiding detection. They had to hunt down Messerschmitts, while being conscious of what was behind them, quickly identify aircraft from nothing more than a black speck, and sometimes turn and face a plane that was pursuing them in order to engage in a dogfight. All of these were technical maneuvres and decisions that had to be taken while flying at high speed. The Germans were also adept at hiding and bouncing, which gave rise to the maxim – 'beware the Hun in the sun'.

Alfred Price concluded that The Hardest Day, despite being a day where both sides lost the greatest number of planes compared to the rest of the Battle of Britain, was not decisive. In a strategic sense, there is some merit to this argument. Clearly, the war was not won on this date, nor was the Battle of Britain itself. However, it did force the Luftwaffe into changing tactics, which weakened their hand. And if we the Few are mostly remembered for their heroism, then the consequences of The Hardest Day can be viewed on those same terms and appreciated for the boon it gave to the Allies. Hitler's first reversal, in a war that had been going his way, is no small thing. The morale of the British was boosted, while German pilots felt a mixture of stress and newfound respect for their British counterparts.

Price also argues that August 18th was more significant than September 15th – Battle of Britain Day – which saw 1,500 planes in the air. The Luftwaffe attacked London in the hope of drawing the RAF out into a battle of annihilation. Unfortunately for Goering's Luftwaffe, German planes were disrupted by serious cloud cover and they failed to cause the English capital any serious damage. The Nazis had been failed by intelligence again, and they were again surprised by the RAF reaction, believing that the British force had been severely depleted. In fact, the RAF were well rested after the Germans had focused on bombing London in Phase 3 of the Battle of Britain.

This blitzing of London forced more than 150,000 people to seek shelter in underground stations on a nightly basis. According to Livia Gershon's *What Life Was Like During The Blitz*, this period exacted a physical toll on the populace, with an increase in ulcers, tics, cerebral haemorrhages, miscarriages and, anxiety attacks. The slogan 'Keep Calm and Carry On' seemed to be effective, however, as only two people a week showed up at hospitals with psychological symptoms.

There is an interesting corollary between the RAF and the blitzed working class. In the underground stations, normal people organized themselves into committees. This spooked the government, who feared the threat of Communism. Nevertheless, reports of working-class solidarity reached the middle and upper classes, and their inherent disdain for the poor was softened, which increased solidarity between the classes. In the RAF, flying prowess had the same effect, and ordinary pilots with a good eye for shooting rubbed shoulders with officers hailing from more salubrious backgrounds.

RAF tactics for the Battle of Britain Day were keenly debated, as they were throughout the Battle of Britain, with some advocating to avoid the war of attrition hoped for by the Nazis by refusing to commit too many planes. Their overriding objective was not to destroy the Luftwaffe, but rather keep them at bay and keep the RAF viable for as long as possible. The Big Wing tactic differed greatly, and the idea here was to meet the Luftwaffe head on and in large groups.

The day itself started with Churchill at the RAF station at Uxbridge, where he ordered the WAAF to relax and act normally, though he had to be asked to stop smoking his signature cigar. The air conditioning simply could not handle it. The radar screens soon picked up enemy planes flying in an aggressive formation. The decision to scramble a response was fraught – it was known if the planes were fighters or bombers, or if they were diversionary force. The decision to scramble turned out to be a good one. Later in the day, Buckingham Palace was partially bombed by a German pilot who crash landed near Victoria Station. He was beaten to so badly by the London crowd, he later died of his wounds.

The British won the Battle of Britain Day, but they exaggerated the number of Germans they had shot down, which goes some way to explaining why this date is seen as significant. For the Germans, their reaction bordered on stupidity; somehow, they saw their loss as proof that the RAF was weakening. Nevertheless, the failure of this attack caused Hitler to cancel Operation Sea Lion for good. Michael White, writing in the *The Guardian*, attributes the failure of this Operation to Hitler's hubris and his ambivalence towards the British, which meant the invasion of Britain was seriously under-planned. It was nothing more than tentative in its aspirations and it was designed to scare Churchill into submitting before any bombs were dropped.

The Luftwaffe never really recovered from losing the Battle of Britain. Ultimately, Bungay attributes to the quality of the British leadership compared to the German one. This is an interesting analysis, and it carries some weight. After all, the Nazis were essentially gangsters, equally concerned with securing their petty power bases as they were with world domination. While there was conflict and personality clashes in the RAF, the Luftwaffe, like other parts of the Nazi apparatus, was run on an adversarial model. Power was best consolidated by leaders who forced their underlings into unhealthy competition. And while the British had strong personalities, the Luftwaffe was run by the corrupt Hermann Goering, a faded World War 1 ace who was now a Yes Man around Hitler.

Churchill was notably hands-on, and he spent his time visiting different airfields and radar stations. Conversely, Hitler cared little for air combat, and his role was far more passive. This may have been a blessing, however, as his tinkering on battlefields later in the war cost the lives of many German soldiers.

Another factor to consider is that of timing. As previously discussed, Operation Sea Lion was little more than an afterthought for Hitler, but the RAF were well-prepared for the Battle of Britain even before it started. Decisions taken throughout the 1930s, by pioneering and far-sighted individuals, such as Dowding and Park, meant that Churchill could draw on good pilots, fast planes and a sophisticated radar network in 1940. This organisation meant that British pilots had a disciplined framework to work with, though there were still significant gaps. The aforementioned Doe felt abandoned during the war, with a noticeable lack of direction from above. Still, because of the German's lack of planning and greater improvisation, Luftwaffe pilots were at a greater disadvantage. This also resulted in greater individualism amongst the German ranks, which led to more reckless actions by pilots in pursuit of glory and less teamwork.

Ultimately, The Hardest Day and the Battle of Britain meant a great deal, even if it did not mean outright victory. On the road to Berlin and the defeat of Hitler, it meant that anti-Fascists could live and fight another day. Without the defense of Biggin Hill and Kenley, for instance, there would have been no hope, either as an abstract feeling or in real terms. People need the will to carry on in daunting circumstances, and the hope furnished from staving off German planes fuelled the war effort in an emotional and moral sense. Furthermore, without the RAF and the WAAF, there would have been no hope of the Americans joining the war, of Normandy, or of the other significant milestones that meant the enlightened world was one step closer to smashing the Swastika. Without the Few, Britain might have dropped out of the war entirely, leaving Europe to be dominated by either the Nazis or the Soviets.

Even Churchill's most exultant words do not come close to describing the debt the world owes to the men and women who stood firm on August 18th and beyond.

Finally, if you enjoyed this book, don't forget to leave an honest review as it helps us tremendously to produce more quality content in the future!

Click here to leave the review

Bibliography

Books

Armitage, Michael, *World War II, Day by Day*, DK Books, 2004

Bell, P. M. H., *Twelve Turning Points of the Second World War*, Yale University Press, 2011

Bishop, Chris, Military Atlas of World War II, Amber Books, 2005

Bergstrom, *The Battle of Britain: An Epic Conflict Revisited*, Casemate Publishers, 2015

Bungay, Stephen, *The Most Dangerous Enemy: A History of the Battle of Britain*, Aurum Press, 2015

Clayton, Tim & Craig, Phil, *Finest Hour: The Battle of Britain*, Simon & Schuster, 1999

Dildy, Douglas C. & Turner, Graham, *Battle of Britain 1940: The Luftwaffe's 'Eagle Attack'*, Osprey Publishing, 2018

Eriksson, Patrick, *Alarmstart: The German Fighter Pilot's Experience in the Second World War: Northwestern Europe - from *the Battle of Britain to the Battle of Germany*, Amberley Publishing, 2019

Korda, Michael, *With Wings Like Eagles: The Untold Story of the Battle of Britain*, Harper Collins, 2009

Price, Alfred, *Battle of Britain: A Summer of Reckoning*, Ian Allan Publishing, 2010

Price Alfred, *The Hardest Day: The Battle of Britain, 18 August 1940*, Phoenix, 1998

Times Atlas of the Second World War II, Rh Value Publishing, 1995

Thompson, Wing Commander H. L., *New Zealanders with the Royal Air Force (VOL. 1)*, Historical Publications Branch, 1953

Townsend, Peter, *Duels of Eagles*, Castle Books, 2003

Warner, Carl, *Life and Death in the Battle of Britain*, Imperial War Museum, 2018

Academic Articles

Cumming, Anthony J., Did Radar Win the Battle of Britain?, *The Historian*, Vol. 69, No. 4 (WINTER 2007)

Isles, Scott Paul, *More than 'an enemy's name, rank and number': Information gained from Luftwaffe prisoners of war and its use for British intelligence during the Battle of Britain, July – October 1940*, Honours Dissertation, 2018

Spaatz, Carl, Leaves from my Battle of Brain Diary, *The Air Power Historian*, Vol. 4, No. 2, (April, 1957)

Newspaper Articles

Battle of Britain: Flypast for 75th anniversary of 'Hardest Day', BBC News, August 18, 2015

Berlin arms factories bombed in three-hour raid, *The Guardian*, August 27, 1940

Bandler, Suri, *The importance of active commemoration of history*, The Tech, February 12, 2015

Cairns, Michael, *Spitfire Paddy: the Irish ace who gave his all in the Battle of Britain*, BBC News, September 15, 2015

Cheers for fighters and A.A. Successes, *The Guardian*, September 15, 1940

Elvery, Martin, *Heroic pilot is remembered on Battle of Britain's 'hardest day'*, Oxford Mail, August 20, 2015

Foxley-Norris, Christopher, *OBITUARY: Group Captain Colin Gray*, Independent, September 30, 1995

Furniss, Elliot, *Lasting tribute to war hero Elizabeth*, East Anglian Daily Times, August 21, 2010

Gershon, Livia, *What Life Was Like During The London Blitz*, JSTOR Daily, August 20, 2018

Group Captain John Carey, fighter pilot, obituary, The Telegraph, December 9, 2004

Kenneally, Ian (Editor), *The Battle of Britain*, The Revolution Papers, June 20, 2017

Miles, Tim, *75th Anniversary of the Battle of Britain: August 18th, 1940 – Kent Remembers the Hardest Day*, Bexley Times, August 18, 2015

Miller, Barbara, *Battle of Britain: Spitfires, Hurricanes take to skies on 75th anniversary of 'Hardest Day'*, ABC News, August 19, 2015

Penfold, Phil, *RAF heroine got a 'man's medal' for courageous role in Battle of Britain*, Daily Record, July 31, 2010

Quinn, Joseph, *Battle of Britain pilot at 100: 'The only advice I can give to people is be Irish'*, Irish Times, July 17, 2019

Rennell, Tony, *Why did we humiliate Polish aces after their Battle of Britain Heroics? How an ungrateful nation wanted to deport men our women fell for and Hitler feared*, Daily Mail, October 29, 2016

Sewell, Katie, *Princess Margaret: Unearthed Letter reveals Pete Townsend split not all it seemed*, Express, May 6, 2020

Sheldrick, Giles, *The Battle of Britain: Aerial salute to bravery of The Few*, Express, August 18, 2015

White, Michael, *Battle of Britain was won as much by German ineptitude as British Heroism*, The Guardian, August 31, 2015

Museum Website

RAF Museum, *Radar – The Battle Winner?*, RAF Museum **https://www.rafmuseum.org.uk/research/online-exhibitions/history-of-the-battle-of-britain/radar-the-battle-winner.aspx**. Accessed: 22/04/20.

YouTube

The Operations Room, *The Hardest Day, Battle of Britain – Time-lapse*, April 2019 (YouTube Video) https://www.youtube.com/watch?v=34KxPpoq7iU. Accessed: 29/04/20.

Printed in Great Britain
by Amazon